BARBERSHOP

POETRY IN MANY STYLES

ERIC LAWRENCE FRAZIER MBA

THE POWER IS NOW MEDIA, INC.
RADIO I TV I MAGAZINE I SEMINARS

CONTENTS

BARBERSHOP
Poetry in Many Styles
By
Eric Lawrence Frazier, MBA

* * *

Thank you for taking the time to order and support my very first poetry collection. I just have one more request. If you could head over to Amazon and leave a 5-star review.

Reviews are the lifeline for any author and this will help other readers find and enjoy my book.

Best,

Eric L. Frazier

SCAN ME

MORE BOOKS BY ERIC LAWRENCE FRAZIER, MBA

Ice Cream (Vol. 1)

Poetry In Many Flavors

Angel's View of Calvary (Vol. 3)

Poetry For the Soul

The Credit Handbook

Change Your Credit Change Your Life

COPYRIGHT

ACKNOWLEDGEMENT

First, I would like to thank God and the inspiration that He provides me to write. I love the Love of God and I am humbled to be saved by his grace and mercy. This book is dedicated to all who know Him and to those who are still searching. May you find Him. I want to thank my beautiful wife Ruby of 39 years. I love you more than words can say. You have been my rock and my greatest cheerleader from the day we first met. There is not a day that goes by that I am not grateful for all you have done and continue to do for our family and me. I can't imagine life without you. Thank you to my for wonderful daughters Jessica, Briana, Erica and Raela. Each one of you holds a special place in my heart. You are powerful, beautiful and highly intelligent women who are doing great things in life. I am very proud of all of you. To my grandchildren Carrah, Chloe and Cameron I love you very much and cannot wait to see the impact you have on the world. To Virgil and Jordan, you are men of God and of valor. I am thankful for the love you have for Briana and Raela and the life you are making together. I love you both and I am proud to be your father-in-law and for the blessing you are to my family. You all inspire me by the very different lives you're living and great things you are accomplishing. I am very proud to be the Patriarch of the family and I love you all very much.

Thank you, Kim Collier, Director of The Power Is Now Publishing. Your daily support, reminders, and expertise in publishing this book have been extremely valuable. I started with a vision and now we are publishing several books. Thank you for staying on me and working with me through the entire process. This book would not have happened without you. Thank you Goldy Ponce, Graphic designer and leader of The Power Is Now Graphic Design team, your amazing eye for design coupled with your ability to implement exactly what I need has resulted in an amazing cover that captures the true essence of this book. To Val Salomaki and Sheila Gilmore, both leaders of our Technology and Marketing team, you are awesome! It is because of your daily support, great work and professionalism that this book and others will receive the attention they deserve. I appreciate your work very much.

To those of you who are reading this book right now, thank you for taking a chance on me, and the time out of your busy life, to read my poetry. I hope you enjoy the book and share it with others.

DEDICATION

Many years ago, I met Greg Linton, a master barber, in a barber shop in Pomona, California. I did not know what a professional haircut looked or felt like until I met Greg. I was hooked after my first haircut. No one else could cut my hair after meeting Greg. In addition to the great haircuts, Greg and I would engage in great conversations, discussions, and even debates. He was an intelligent and articulate brother, and we became great friends. Sometimes we would just listen to the conversations of others in the room and join their conversation while he was cutting my hair.

He eventually moved and started a barbershop in his home. Over the course of a decade, we developed a very close relationship. I was inspired by the incredible wisdom he would dispense and by his ability to engage and talk freely about the challenges he was facing at the time or the challenges in the world that we would talk about and try to solve. I enjoyed the combination of the privacy of his home and the atmosphere of a barbershop. It was a very therapeutic experience and I always received a great haircut. I dedicate this book to Greg Linton. He no longer cuts hair, but he was one of the best barbers I have ever known.

PREFACE

I remember going to the barbershop with my father and loving it. Other kids would be there, and we would all listen to the conversations of the barbers and patrons about sports, religion, crime, politics, and God knows what else—even women and sex.

There were no limitations on what could be discussed in the barbershop. It was always an educational experience, and I could not get enough of it. It was the highlight of my week to go to the barbershop. It still is today. There is nothing like getting cleaned up, edged up, at the barbershop and looking good for work or play.

Thirty years ago, sitting in the barbershop, I was moved by the environment and the conversations taking place like never before. There was so much engagement, love, camaraderie, and fellowship in the room that I felt like I was among family and friends. No one walking into the barbershop would walk by a barber without getting a high five, a fist bump, or sometimes a hug. It was like a family reunion even, though we were all just there to get a haircut.

The environment in the room and the advice that was being given inspired me. So, I began to write, and it was as if something came over me. I sat down in the waiting area and wrote the poem "Barbershop" in one sitting. I did not even get up to go to the bathroom because I could not stop writing. I came to get a haircut, but when I started writing the poem, my pen just would not stop moving. People were telling me it was my turn, but I told them to go ahead. I did not get my haircut that day, but I finished the poem.

When I finished writing the poem, I shared it with my barber and everyone else in the room and they were all inspired by it. "Barbershop" is one of my favorite poems of all time; even today, three decades after my barbershop experiences, it still moves me.

Barbershops are not the same today as I remember them back then. There is not the same degree of fellowship and camaraderie now. Many people come in and just sit, wait, and not engage the person waiting next to them. The shops are playing music that sometime may not be suitable for children—and not everyone is into underground rap or trap music. I had a barber that would come to my home to cut my hair on a Monday morning. We would have great conversations about life, and he would take his time and give me a fantastic haircut. Unfortunately, Covid 19 ended that so I am back in the shop. The Barbara Shop I have been going to since I arrived in downtown Riverside California almost 20 years ago is called Cold Cutz. They are all talented barbers who will keep you current with the latest trends in black hair. John Jefferson has been the proprietor for over 20 years and is a Master Barber. Go see him if you need a cold cut.

~Eric Lawrence Frazier, Poet

WHAT I'M THANKFUL FOR

As I get older and wiser
Things become clearer to me,
Because God has gradually given me
The maturity to see,
That I am at least as much a sinner now
As I was when He saved me.

That I am more the sinner now
Than what I thought myself to be.
What a paradox to see
That in my relationship with Christ
I see the sinner in me.
Yet, He sees me as righteous and holy.

. . .

My practical reality is that I am a greater sinner

Than I thought I would ever be,

As I try to imitate Jesus

And follow the Word he has given me.

I realize more today,

What a condemned creature I would be,

If it were not for His death,

That paid for all my sins unselfishly,

And His blood that cleanses and makes me holy,

And His resurrection mixed

With my faith that has regenerated me,

To live in eternity with God, who is my destiny.

And so I rely on His promises

And the Word that I have been set free,

Even though it is this very Word

That shines the light on sinner me.

I am thankful that I am truly set free

From sin and condemnation by Jesus only.

He has paid my debt

And completed my work for me, wholly.

.   .   .

As I get older and wiser things appear clearly,

I am utterly dependent on Jesus to steer me.

The harder I try to be perfect,

And free from impropriety,

The more I realize that I am still trapped

In that psychological fallacy,

That following God's Word exactly,

Is what makes me perfect and free,

And not faith in Jesus only.

So, on this bright Thanksgiving Day,

I thank God for His gift of grace and mercy,

Without which I would have no hope

To live eternal, and sin-free.

Even though, I see the sin in me,

I live by faith in Jesus only,

and not by faith in me.

THE GREAT I AM

I am in the image of the great I AM.

I AM male and female.

I AM alpha and omega.

I AM light and darkness.

I AM joy and fear.

I AM loved and despised.

I AM strength and weakness.

I HAVE formed you out of the dust of the earth.

I HAVE breathed into your nostrils the breath of life.

I HAVE created the sun and moon, earth and star.

I AM the host of heaven.

I AM the omnipotent.

. . .

I AM the great I AM and there is none other before Me.

I AM the image of you and you are the image of Me.

Male and female you were made to be

Vessels of life and the essence of Me.

I AM has given you wisdom and knowledge,

Grace and stature,

Power and strength,

Peace and love,

Joy and happiness,

I AM has made you who you are.

Whatever you might be is because of the great I AM.

I AM abides in you and you in the great I AM.

Every step you make the great I AM already takes.

Moment by moment you begin to see

How the great I AM lives in thee.

Life, consciousness, Cosmic awareness, and mother earth.

I AM is in the trees that point to the center of the universe.

I AM is in the winds that carry his praises and spread the seeds of life.

I AM is in the water that holds life in the body and fish in the sea.

I AM is in plant and animal life that roams free.

I AM is in the moon and stars whose brightness we see.

I AM is in life coming into existence,

The birth coming from the womb,

The seed springing from the ground,

The soul rising from the body to eternity.

I AM is the power of life.

Nothing exists without the great I AM.

Everything that exists is within the great I AM.

Everything and everywhere is under control of the great I AM.

The political, social, historical, economical, judicial, and spiritual realm

Are subject to the great I AM.

The rich, powerful, intellectual, influential, and wealthy,

Are subject to the great I AM.

The kings, queens, presidents and prime ministers, dictators,

And emperors are all subject to the great I AM.

I AM created Adam and Eve and banished them from the garden.

I AM walked with Enoch and translated him to heaven.

I AM spoke to Noah and had favor on his family

and saved them from a watery death.

I AM spoke with Moses from a burning bush and led Israel free from captivity.

. . .

I AM spoke through Elijah and translated him by a chariot of fire.

I AM is the charismatic prophets of old,

Whose proclamation brought judgment and miraculous occurrences.

I AM anointed King David and promised his seed would give birth to the Messiah.

I AM so loved the world that he clothed himself

With the flesh of humanity

And tabernacled among us.

I AM became a living sacrifice meant for death.

I AM is justice and death is his atonement.

I AM is love and justification unmerited.

I AM is peace between man and the great I AM reconciled.

I AM is love clothed with flesh meant for death.

Love yourself through the great I AM.

In loving yourself, you love the great I AM.

In loving yourself, you see the great I AM in every human being.

In loving yourself, you will begin to love all men everywhere.

Because the great I AM loves you.

The great I AM abides in you,

And you are the image of the great I AM.

Why then, my brother, do you kill one another?

Death cannot kill your brother because he is eternal.

The essence and the image of the I AM.

Why then attempt to kill the great I AM,

The author of death and life and creator of man.

The image and essence of your own being and man.

Death is freedom in the great I AM.

Freedom from time and being present is in the great I AM.

Freedom from sickness and old age is in the great I AM.

Death is the agent of the great I AM.

To deliver us to our destiny with eternity.

Let the great I AM bring this freedom to your brother,

While you wait for your own freedom,

Through the power and love of the great I AM.

You, my brother, are the image of the great I AM.

Peace is in the great I AM.

Love is in the great I AM.

Love the great I AM,

Embrace the great I AM,

Know the great I AM,

And know who YOU really ARE.

DON'T LIE TO YOURSELF

I'm going *to* do this,
    I'm going to do that,
I'm going to lose weight,
But here I sit getting fat.
Don't lie to yourself.

I'm going to work hard,
I'm going to work smart,
I'm going to meet my commitments,
But here I am in the mall with a shopping cart.
Don't lie to yourself.

I'm going to start school,
I'm going to finish my degree,

I'm going to do all my homework,

But here I sit watching TV.

Don't lie to yourself.

I'm going to spend more time home

I'm going to cook once a week

I'm going to help clean up around the house

But here I sit still at home quiet as a mouse.

Don't lie to yourself.

I'm going to show more appreciation to my wife.

I'm going to have date night.

I'm going to surprise her with frequent gifts of appreciation.

But here I sit by myself at a convention.

Don't lie to yourself.

Stop talking about what you are going to do.

Start doing what you know to do.

The road to hell is filled with good intentions.

The road to heaven Is to be present.

Where declarations are not required,

And everything you need to do, no matter,

The circumstances will be revealed to you.

Don't lie to yourself.

ACCEPTANCE

I want acceptance,

You want acceptance,

Everybody wants acceptance.

Inequality, social justice, racial profiling, police brutality.

This is our daily realty, chronicled on the news nightly.

We can't seem to catch a break, for Christ's sake,

If you are alive and walking or driving, you may catch a case.

Irrespective of our age, or gender, it's all about our color.

Caught up in Criminal Justice system no father or mother.

Locked up for years, your family crying tears,

No justice, no peace, no comfort near.

Just do the time and we will be here.

I can't get acceptance without being on the take.

If it is not my color or class, it's my lack of cash.

I have to buy acceptance and that is just as bad.

Followed in the grocery store,

Ignored in the jewelry store,

Can't get help in the shoe store,

Watched like a hawk in the department store.

Trying to get acceptance if you're poor.

Will only have the merchants,

Showing you the door.

Get a little money.

And everybody will start treating you funny.

You'll think you have arrived,

But to them you probably stole the money.

The only acceptance you can count on.

Is what you get when you have been reborn.

It is the norm when you are in the family of the reborn.

They accept you because they have been accepted by God.

Who sent His beloved Son to die.

And if you are wondering why?

So that you can have unconditional love and acceptance:

Acceptance regardless of your color,

Acceptance even if you are a brother,

Acceptance regardless of your money,

Acceptance even if you look funny.

Acceptance regardless of your class,

Acceptance even if your English lacks,

Acceptance regardless of your education,

Acceptance if you skipped graduation,

Acceptance regardless of your spirituality,

Acceptance even if you do not meet their standard of morality.

I thank God that He has accepted me.

Even though I'm just a pile of mud,

I have been accepted out of pure love from above.

Not from man who has never had the capacity for love.

To accept me like the God above without any conditions.

Or the requirements of a prestigious club.

. . .

God's only reason for accepting me is out of pure love.

I want acceptance, you want acceptance,

Everybody wants acceptance.

I want acceptance, you want acceptance.

I thank God for the acceptance He has given.

RESTORATION

I see my brother crying out in desperation,

    Broken and in the depths of despair he desires restoration.

Ready to give up and to no longer care,

He begins to wonder if God is even there,

And his brothers and sisters, who are supposed to care,

Forget that Jesus said his burdens they would bear.

I see my brother overwhelmed and full of hopelessness,

Consumed by the troubles he has created through carelessness.

Now disheartened by his own weakened flesh,

He is grieved by his own sinfulness created by lust.

Full of contrition, he wants absolution through confession.

But has forgotten that Jesus' propitiation brought his redemption.

And that his faith in Him imparts justification.

And what he really needs is restoration.

He does not need your sin inspection or self-righteous patronization.

He needs communication, compassion, and revitalization.

He needs to apprehend your love and God's salvation.

You see, what he is suffering from is spiritual starvation.

That leads to spiritual malnutrition.

He needs the kind of support and relief that can come from the congregation,

People who have compassion, who are not always for self-satisfaction,

People who have the capacity to love and to show love,

Instead of always being the ones who need to be loved.

People who want to help and really care,

Instead of people who say they care.

But never a burden will they bear.

Oh, I pray for my brothers and sisters out there!

For we all struggle with the prince of the air.

Overwhelmed and overtaken by many things in the world that be,

I am careful not to judge with self-righteous glee.

Because I know in my heart it could be me.

Anybody can be drawn into sinful obsessions,

Make mistakes that lead to devastation,

Find themselves in bondage to addiction.

And without help will never see spiritual emancipation.

You can become desperate in your situation.

And need God's people to bring about restoration.

The alternative is to leave them in a difficult position.

Where they drink strong libations to cope with depression,

Or take drugs to escape, looking for higher alleviations,

Only to find further degradation and depression in this worldly
Matriculation.

While brothers and sisters are suffering from spiritual starvation,

Or long incarcerations, family disputations, economic devastation,

Abortions and personal humiliation, the church has gone on a
spiritual Vacation.

Bear your brother's burden and become ministers of restorations.

It is part of God's plan of salvation and message of reconciliation.

We should share it with every soul in the world.

And practice it in the congregation.

ATTITUDE

We've all heard the saying,

That attitude is everything,

And that attitude affects your altitude.

I would concur with both statements,

But there is something else I think you should consider.

Having a great and positive attitude

Is critical to your success in life.

and in business.

A poor attitude.

Can affect your interpersonal relationships.

At home, school, or the workplace,

And can potentially be the primary cause.

For an improper response to a relative,

Neighbor, customer, employee, or boss.

Ultimately, it will have an adverse effect.

On your effectiveness as a person,

leader, father, and witness for Christ.

What is so unique about a positive attitude,

Is that it is something that everyone can have.

And yet, you cannot get it at the best university,

You cannot get it from the greatest parents in the world,

No one can force it on you, nor can you buy it.

You see, what is so special about a positive attitude.

Is that it is something that resides in us all.

And we decide to turn it on or off.

A positive attitude is a decision.

A decision that should be made

Despite whatever challenges life holds

In store for you each day.

A decision is not subject

To predetermined events,

Or dictated by the attitude of others.

. . .

When you wake up in the morning,

The first decision you make,

Among the numerous decisions you will make,

Before you even leave home,

Is whether to be a positive influence,

And source of motivation for others,

Or a negative influence and source of anxiety for others.

It is a critical decision that only you can make today,

And it will affect everyone else around you...wife,

Husband, father, mother, sister, brother,

Employee, boss, student, teacher, neighbor, and friend.

Make a decision to be positive today,

And every day as you work very hard,

To achieve positive results for your life,

And your business and family,

In your pursuit of excellence.

STRANGE PEOPLE

*L*ife is strange and people are stranger.

I believe whenever there are people there is danger,

Especially those you thought you knew,

Who surprise you, without even a clue,

As to how strange they are by the evil they do,

And in that instant, you realize,

They are complete strangers to you.

They do things you would not do,

And say things you would not say,

And are quick to turn against you,

If you refuse the games they play.

Then the danger comes full sway,

Because they perceive you as their enemy,

Someone who might get in the way.

Avoid them. Let the players play.

They will reap what they sow, because God really knows,

The heartache, pain, and suffering that they bestow,

On people they call their friends ,

And on people they do not even know.

911

The sun and moon look the same to liberty today.
    Day has become night,
And night has become death on September 11th.

Lady Liberty wept as she witnessed an assault on her city
By iron eagles Turned into missiles,
Of death and destruction.

She stood paralyzed by surprise, unable to alert the city,
And could only watch in horror,
As the eagles flew straight into her twin brothers:
Freedom and Capitalism.

Her twin brothers have stood tall and proud,

With her overlooking the city,

But Freedom turned to marshal law,

And Capitalism came to a sudden halt,

As her brothers were destroyed

By the eagles' impact and began to crumble to earth.

The force of the impact and intensity of the fire,

Turned her twin brothers into a mountain of,

Dust, ash, and a tomb,

For six thousand children of Liberty.

Servants of Liberty came to rescue her children,

But the fires engulfed them.

Many died bravely trying to rescue,

Others trapped beneath and between,

The crumbling concrete and twisted iron.

Their lungs filled with the dust,

And ash that filled the atmosphere,

Their bodies fell into a grave of mass destruction,

But their souls ascended to safety with God,

And their courage and love of humanity remain with us for eternity.

Lady Liberty's foundation shook as fear took over her city,

And mourning and wailing filled the air.

. . .

Lady Liberty wailed as the stench of death rose to her nostrils,

And the cries for help penetrated her concrete ears.

Lady Liberty cried for her children as they jumped to their death,

Filling the streets below with pools of blood.

The legacy of her twin brothers for now is only,

Darkness and ash that covers her in shame.

But they will rise again.

Lady Liberty has been brought to this low estate on this day,

But she has not been defeated.

She stomps her feet and stretches,

forth her hand promising a new day.

Where Freedom and Liberty will rise again, and justice will prevail.
The sun and moon look the same to Liberty today.

Day has become night and night has become death.

On September 11th.

But a new day is coming,

And we will never forget.

ONE DAD

They say you only have one Dad,

   Just like there is only one God,

Just like there is only one Lord,

Just like there is only one Spirit.

It is interesting to see how one,

Anything makes it incredibly special.

God out of love,

Gave his one and only begotten Son.

God is the love of my life,

Because God is the essence of love.

The Lord is the savior of my life,

Because He purchased it with His life,

The Spirit is the seal of my life,

And He guarantees eternal life.

But you, Dad,

Are the reason I have life.

Your life is the reason I have life.

You instilled in me a desire to live life to its fullest.

Life with no boundaries or limitations,

Life with dreams realized,

And dreams to still achieve.

You helped me to succeed in life,

To be in life what you hoped,

and dreamed would be right.

Therefore, on your birthday,

I celebrate life,

Because you have made life special.

You gave me life; you nurture it,

And now I love life,

As I have always loved you.

Thank you for life,

For love, and for your love and life.

Happy Birthday, Dad!

TIRED

I am so tired, so very tired ,
          That I do not know what to do!
Do you know what I'm saying?

Neck hurting, eyes drooping,
Struggling to stay awake,
Head in hand, holding up my head,
I Wish I could take a nap.

Rubbing my neck and closing my eyes,
Breathing in deeply and making big sighs,
Aching bones, tired and swollen feet,
Shoes so tight my toes feel the heat.

. . .

Leaning forward and backward

And walking side to side,

My speech is so slurred,

I sound like I'm talking jive!

I tried to sing myself awake,

But the melody didn't take.

I turned up the radio to arrest my attention,

But my mind was too focused,

On sleep deprivation.

I'm so tired,

That if you looked up the word in the dictionary,

You would see a picture of me!

Lying in a soft feather bed, resting my head and feet,

Getting some needed sleep,

And dreaming about a future and adventure.

I'm so tired that the last three letters,

Of the word are the color of my eyes.

I'm so tired, so VERY tired

That I don't know what to do!

I'm going to find my bed, put a pillow over my head,

And play like I am dead.

You DO know what I'm saying, don't you?

THE BARBERSHOP

In the barber's shop, there is a sanctuary,

a haven, a temple where men of all races, ages,

and backgrounds gather together to escape for a few hours.

It is the central nervous system of the community.

It is the gatekeeper of gossip and rumor and the rendezvous,

For social and intellectual exchange.

In the barber's shop there is an old sage,

A master barber whose reputation is known,

In all circles of the city.

He dispenses wisdom and knowledge,

He exudes empathy and sympathy,

And he passionately exhorts and admonishes,

As he creates works of art on the heads of his patrons.

Everybody comes to the barber's shop,

If they want to know or be known.

They come from every walk of life.

From the mountaintops of success,

To valleys of poverty and despair.

They are the tired and the oppressed,

The downtrodden and beaten,

The depressed and the unemployed,

The lost and the broken.

They are preachers and teachers,

Lawyers and leaders, the entrepreneur

And the drug dealer.

They are the bankers and doctors,

White-collar and blue-collar workers,

The educated and uneducated.

They are the tall and the short,

The fat and skinny,

The light- and dark-skinned,

And occasionally the white-skinned.

From all walks of life, they come to the temple,

The sanctuary, the barber's shop,

To counsel and to receive counsel,

To feel and to be felt, to hear and to be heard,

To cry and to cry for others, to vent and to relax,

To confess and to repent.

Even to sell and to buy watches and fake gold,

clothing and shoes that are funky and bold.

They come to know and to be known.

In the love and the unity

Of manhood, brotherhood, fatherhood, and sonhood.

They come to know and to be known in the fellowship.

Of those who have understood the challenges

Of growing up black and in the hood.

In the barber's shop they seek refuge

From the paradigms that societies,

Family, work, and God have thrust upon them.

They come to look and listen to others.

Just like them who embrace the love and camaraderie of manhood.

. . .

In the barber's shop,

They sit quietly waiting for their turn.

To sit on the sage's throne of wisdom and knowledge.

Not to dispense it, but to receive it.

Surrounded by life experiences.

That surpass their own limited history,

They are led by an old sage,

That sets the tone for their spiritual,

Intellectual, and emotional journey on the throne,

As He provokes dialogue from the waiting gallery to the throne.

In the barber's shop,

The wisdom and theological expositions,

Of the old sage sends everyone to a realm,

Of thought and philosophical ecstasy,

That their mundane lives have not given them,

Opportunity to contemplate.

They listen attentively as the old sage,

Challenges them on the weighty topics of life and death,

Love and marriage, friendship, and business,

Sports and entertainment, philosophy, and theology,

Faith and God.

. . .

In the barber's shop,

They listen and question, they argue and debate,

They comment and answer,

They challenge and get challenged,

And while their minds have been engaged,

To a realm of thought far above their immediate circumstances,

They do not realize how far this old sage has come for them today.

This old sage - high school dropout, GED sage.

Former gangbanger and drug user,

Former thief and criminal,

Former player and womanizer.

This old sage - poet and itinerant minister,

Youth leader and child counselor,

Husband and father of three,

Life coach and spiritual advisor.

This old sage has come a long way.

His life experiences and words of wisdom,

Are far beyond his chronological age.

He speaks at times as if he has been here before,

Or has been privy to conversations you have had,

With you or your wife.

This old sage has arrested their attention,

For a moment from the problems and issues of life,

That drew them to his sanctuary,

And at the same time, he cuts lines and edges,

Shades and fades, creates curls and add colors.

To oddly shaped heads and faces,

Without missing a point or losing a train of thought.

He is a master barber and a wise old sage.

That can handle the diverse and burden-laden humanity,

That is drawn to his sanctuary.

In the barber's shop,

There are big heads and small heads,

Hook heads and round heads,

Straight hair and curly hair,

Black hair and gray hair,

Bald heads and nappy heads.

There are beards and mustaches,

Clean-shaven faces and unshaven faces.

Everyone is seeking a seat in this sanctuary,

This temple and haven of rest.

There are criminals and liars,

Fornicators and adulterers,

Idolaters and even devil worshippers.

There is no disrespect of persons in the barber's shop,

Come whosoever will and you will be served.

All men seek a moment of rest,

From the mess, they have created with their lives.

They seek the wisdom of the sage,

And of the men who have walked in their shoes,

And have grown out of them.

For in the barber's shop there is wisdom,

There is love, there is fellowship,

And life-changing bonds that will never be broken.

In the barber's shop,

They sit in awe receiving life-changing content,

In context and without pretext.

They watch this old sage,

And master barber turn nappy heads,

And unshaven faces into works of art,

While listening to his dissertations,

And the dialogue of others,

That penetrates their hearts,

And brings about enlightenment,

And new resolutions.

Michelangelo has nothing on this artist and sage,

For he only created art on dead canvasses,

And nonliving things and not skillful masterpieces

Out of living matter on the scalps of humanity,

While at the same time engaging young and old minds

And changing their lives.

In the barber's shop there is wise counsel,

That is why they call it the temple.

In the barber's shop there is peace,

That is why they call it the sanctuary.

In the barbers' shop there is rest,

That is why they call it the haven.

Therefore, to the sages and master barbers who serve humanity,

Whose skill and creativity add beauty to earthen vessels owned
by God,

Whose wisdom and knowledge are poured into those who have been,
Honored to sit upon their throne in the temple,

Whose haven of rest has provided a forum for men from every clime
to come together,

I say with the utmost gravity and sincerity, thank you,

For you are God's servants and His messengers of mercy and grace to
men everywhere.

STAND AND NOT RUN

*L*ord, You know what's in my heart.
Lord, You know my every thought.
Lord, I know my soul You have bought.

I belong to You and You love me too.

There is nothing in this life that can separate me,

From Your love that covers and comforts completely.

Not death because you gave me life,

Not life because it is hidden in Christ,

Not angels because they protect me,

Nor demons because they have no power over me,

Not the future, because you are always present.

Or anything that may come.

. . .

Lord, You have called to me to stand and not run!

And – so - I - stand – Lord!

Because You meet all my needs,

I stand – Lord!

Your power rests in me.

I stand – Lord!

Your name makes the devil flee,

He is defeated, and I have the victory!

Lord, You have called me to stand and not run.

Lord, You know what's in my heart.

Lord, You know my every thought.

Lord, I know my soul You have bought.

I belong to You,

And You love me too.

And – so - I - stand – Lord!

Because You love me,

Taking my place on Calvary,

Suffering pain and agony,

Experiencing death that was meant for me.

I - stand – Lord!

. . .

Because You know me,

You know what's in my heart,

You know my every thought,

And my soul You have bought,

I stand because the enemy has lost,

I stand because You paid the cost,

I stand because outside of You there in none,

Lord you have called me to stand! And I will not run!

DEATH'S REALITY

The death of your father
Wakes you up to the harsh reality,
That you too are going to die.

It robs you of your innocence about life,
And the fantasy of never having a death cry.

It sends you into a tailspin of questions,
Like "Where is he?" and "Why, oh why?"

It causes you to sense a stronger presence.
Of God in your life,
And the need to know the truth,
Instead of believing a lie.

. . .

Is he in hell or in heaven alive?

Can he see me, hear me, touch me?

Or communicate with me even though he died?

He is face to face with Jesus or the devil himself?

Does he now live-in eternal bliss?

Or am I just full of myself?

All these years I have been going to church,

And singing about hope and eternal salvation.

Thirty-four years later,

I stand here today hopeless.

I wonder about my own salvation.

Death confronts your doubts or fears,

About your life's destination.

You are forced to remove them quickly.

Any flawed thinking or crazy expectations,

And the reality that in this life

You may not see the resurrection.

Death wakes you up to the harsh reality,

That you too are going to die.

No longer do you plan to live forever,

Or even see Jesus coming in the sky.

All you have now is fear and an abundance of tears,

That ask the questions of why.

Some are for how he suffered and died,

Others are for questioning God's lack of intervention.

Death changes you forever.

It puts God in the mix of all your conversations.

You now measure the risk of all your endeavors,

No longer are the jokes about death clever,

And your relationship with a God,

A half-hearted endeavor.

Death wakes you up to all the possibilities.

Of how your life on earth is not forever,

That in a moment you are here and the next thing you know.

All of your plans have been severed.

What was important here on earth, what was planned,

What was being worked on is now all gone,

God said it was not important enough to delay taking you home,

It is now time to deal with Me.

And to make heaven or hell your eternal home.

Death wakes you up to the harsh reality.

That you too are going to die.

It robs you of your innocence about life.

And the fantasy of never having a death cry.

It causes you to want to know the truth.

Instead of believing a lie.

I know the truth, but the pain does not go away.

I believe in grace and that by faith we are all saved.

But I can't stop asking the question,

Of why God took my Dad away.

The mental pictures I have of him,

in a casket tortures me night and day.

I know he is not there, but the questions rob me of my sleep.

To live by faith and not by sight,

had been a subject I love to teach,

Until the day my Dad died,

And caused me to check my spiritual belief.

Now I know why ignorance is bliss,

And that faith to some is just fantasy.

Death wakes you up to the harsh reality,

That you too are going to die.

So get your things in order and be ready to die,

Or to see Jesus coming in the sky because it is reality.

Say "I love you" every day to your family and friends,

Because you never know the day it is all going to end.

Worship God every day and thank him for the grace he lends.

HELP ME, MY BROTHER

Help me, my brother,

If you catch me in a sin.

Come to me gently

And let me know I cannot win.

Help me, my brother,

To carry each other's burden

So we may not be tempted.

and both have a new beginning.

Help me, my brother,

. . .

To remember that we all fall short,

And none of us are exempted.

We do not judge but provide support,

Help me, my brother,

To take pride in myself,

Instruct me in the way,

to be centered and not right or left,

Help me, my brother,

To understand the things that I should.

To tie into the Lord and trust in his Word,

I know that Satan is waiting and ready,

To cut my cord.

(Based on Galatians 6: 1-6)

TV REMOTE

It used to be mine but now it's Ruby's.
Every night she takes the remote control,
and asks me what I want to watch,
But watches what she wants to watch anyway.

I look like Scooby Do saying "I don't know",
Because I really don't know what I want to watch
But I do know that I want to flip the channels.
I want the remote control.

I don't know what happened.
I would lay in the bed or sit on the couch,
With my remote firmly in my hand.
She waits until I leave the room, grabs it, does not,

give it back!

I ask politely for the remote control and she says, no

I am the captain now— so take that!

Who gave her control over the programs or shows?

Who made her the boss over the remote control?

This is whack.

She has crossed the line,

Of a special territory and rights of all men

To control the remote control.

I want it back!

I am Patriarch, not guest,

And, THIS, my poetic protest!

WHY I DON'T NEED MUSIC IN
MY CAR

Sometimes I do not need to hear the vocals of a woman
or man,

Or string instruments strung by the hand,

Or bass drums beat by the foot,

Or wind instruments that make music from the lips.

I just want to ride,

Listening to the hump of the tires on the road

Or the wind blowing against the windshield,

that tell stories untold.

The sounds of horns blowing on the highway,

The sound of screeching tires throughout the day

And most of all I want to hear me think.

. . .

I want to hear me think about life – its failures and victories.

I want to hear me think about conversations - past and present.

I want to hear me think about achieving goals – my wish that what I touch Turns to gold.

I just wanna ride.

Thinking about my family, my girls, my wife, my life,

And how I can stay strong to do what is right.

I don't need to hear any music about strife,

Holy wars about who's right,

About a nine-year-old taking a life with a knife,

Or being a gang banger and growing up in the hood

And how bad is now good.

I just wanna ride,

And think about the sunny side,

Watch the moon ride the darkness,

The city lights,

The beautiful sight,

And gain insight.

I just wanna ride.

THE POOT

Foul, pungent, rotten, spoiled air
From the gaseous bowels of you know where,
People in the world who just do not care,
About your right to breathe pleasant or normal air.

The rotten smell sneaks up on you like a thief in the night.
And at first you wonder if it is you,
But the smell just isn't right,
So you close your mouth and nose tight.

Now unable to breathe you are forced to take flight.
You try to think if you ever smelt anything so bad,
A rotten egg or spoiled food in the garbage bag,

Whatever it was it almost made you gag.

The nerve of some people who can't hold but pass,

Their foul, pungent, rotten gas.

TOILET PAPER

I'm sitting on the toilet writing poetry.

I don't know why.

I guess it has got to come out of me

Like everything else. Is it me or my butt?

Writing words as I evacuate

The substance from my gut.

Am I now clear to think?

Even though I am surrounded by stink!?

I don't know why I am doing this.

Maybe I am crazy or just too lazy

To sit down at a desk or computer.

What I do know is that I need an air freshener.

Who Wee!

MY CONSCIENCE, MY COMPASS

*T*he compass of my soul is the conscience I behold;

And, oh, how my body has taken a toll when my,

Conscience has been put on hold!

The whispers in my head that say "No"

Are countered by my body that wants to go.

My soul cries out "Oh no,"

I'm in a struggle for my life again, "Here we go!"

The spirit of God speaks to my spirit,

And my conscience is strengthened.

It speaks louder and louder the truth,

And what's right, the good and the light.

. . .

But my body closes my ears and my eyes tight,

So that I will not see the light or hear what's right.

My body wants blindness and death,

But my conscience fights for life.

My soul cries out, but my body says that's alright,

Go ahead and do it: you'll feel better tonight.

Oh conscience, oh conscience,

Where are you now that I have met my carnal need?

And wow I can't hear you anymore!

I can't feel you anymore!

I can't see you anymore

All because you were ignored.

My spirit is quenched, and my conscience is seared.

My faith is all but gone and my eyes welled with tears.

My soul is distressed because my conscience is no longer near.

Was it worth it to lose my soul and the world to gain,

By ignoring my conscience, the result is I now live-in pain.

Lord restore my faith so that my conscience I might regain,

I need to live my life in this world and not go insane.

PEOPLE SAY

People say things but don't mean it.

    People think things but won't say it.

People do things then regret it.

People lie about things then try to fix it.

People forgive but never forget it.

People love but never get enough of it.

People hate and never come to grips with it.

People hurt and may never get over it.

People die, and their families have to deal with it.

People cry because they have no immediate answer.

People live because they find joy doing it.

People sleep because their mind is at peace with it.

People say and do many things and don't mean it.

Knowing and understanding God's purpose

For our lives is the only way to stop it.

POVERTY

*R*oaches scattering across the kitchen floor.

No food is in the house and we are dirt poor.

Daddy is asleep and Mama's up watching him snore.

The baby is wet and crying and his behind is sore.

Six kids cramped into one bedroom.

Our uncle's stone drunk

And stinking up the room.

He's sleeping on the floor

And we are in the bunk beds.

No one has a pillow

But their hands under their heads.

Up in the morning and we all smell like pee.

The sheets are all wet and our draws

Are drooping to our knees.

Get cleaned up everybody,

Our sleepless momma said.

Come and get your breakfast

And comb your nappy heads.

Off to school with our lunch bags in hand,

We were the poorest little kids in ghetto-land.

All we ever wanted was to just fit in,

To be like the other kids and have many friends.

But poverty has a way of making you stick out,

You're not very happy, all you do is pout,

Even though it's hard you do grow up and out

From the depth of poverty to working class clout.

If I could live my life over again,

I would grow up a rich kid maybe then become a kingpin.

But I know that it's impossible to live life over again

And that I should be grateful that my journey has yet to end.

Who knows what I will do with this life of mine,

Considering the experiences, I have had

And the wisdom that has come with time.

This I do know, with all my heart and soul,
That God has brought me here so far
Up from the struggle, from low to high bar
And HE has helped me reach my every goal.

MY ME

∞

My life,
My way, my tears, my fears, my love,

My hate, my weakness, my strength, my cool,

My hot, my anger, my calm, my glut, my want,

My worry, my confidence, my jealousy, my security,

My sadness, my happiness, my lost, my found,

My memory, my forgetfulness, my forgiveness, my grudge,

My peace, my turmoil, my joy, my despair, my happiness,

My frustration, my favorite, my enemy, my worst,

My best, my courage, my fear, my debt, my assets,

My wealth, my poverty, my benevolence, my covetousness,

My fight, my reconciliation, my payback, my let it go,

My sickness, my health, my heart, my mind, my eyes,

My soul, my hair, my vanity, my skin, my identity,

My color, my plight, my clothes, my message,

My shoes, my statement, my feet, my hands, my toes,

My fingers, my legs, my arms, my face, my nose, my lips,

My teeth, my forehead, my wrinkles, my ears, my lobes,

My beard, my mustache, my cheeks, my butt,

My sexuality, my head, my mind, my thoughts,

My depression, my exaggerations, my lies, my stories, my sermons,

My motivation, my lessons, my house, my car, my dog,

My bed, my wife, my children, my friends, my neighbors,

My pastor, my employees, my employer, my boss, my goals,

My plans, my trips, my vacations, my money, my time, my wine,

My beer, my Hennessy, my grey goose, my watermelon, my
strawberries,

My oranges, my grits, my bacon, my eggs over easy,

My ham, my fried chicken, my corn bread, my collard greens,

My black-eyed peas, my homemade soups, my noodles, my shrimp,

My catfish, my burritos, my tacos, my deep-fried fish,

. . .

My refried beans, my cheese, my ice cream,

My oatmeal and raisin cookies, my basketball, my golf,

My racquetball, my bike, my running, my exercise, my beach,

My sand, my ocean, my pool, my putting green, my theater,

My movies, my music, my phone, my tablet, my CDs,

My laptop, my online radio, my people, my history, my country,

My president, my Jesus, my God,

My Holy Spirit, my eternity, my destiny,

My death.

HOME-OWNERSHIP

*omeownership brings stability.

To individuals and families who have never

Had a dwelling place that they could call their own.

There is something special about real estate

That is unlike anything else on earth you can possess.

Real estate you own is not a like a car,

That will decay over time and you have to replace it.

Real estate you own is not like clothes that go out of style,

And you have to buy new ones.

Real estate you own is not like expensive vacations,

Or experiences that only last a moment in time.

. . .

Real estate you own is not like an apartment,

Where the landlords increase the rent until it's unaffordable.

Real estate you own is not like staying at your parent's house,,

Where you know you can't stay forever.

Homeownership is the beginning of wealth,

Wealth that increases over time,

Becomes your estate and legacy.

Homeownership is the pride of a mother nurturer,

The kitchen is her domain.

Homeownership is the pride of a father,

Provider and protector of his territory and family.

Homeownership is the foundation of permanence,

And the place where life happens,

Birthdays are celebrated, and death is mourned.

Homeownership is the place where you build memories.

Memories that can never be taken from you,

Etched in walls and concrete,

Experienced in rooms and floors,

And living in trees and shrubs planted by your hand.

. . .

Howe-ownership is the manifestation of you - your style,

Your colors, your smell, your stuff, your junk,

Your memories, your yard, and your spaces, your life.

It's the height markers on your first child's bedroom wall.

It's the hearts drawn in the concrete slabs,

When you poured your patio floor.

It's the birthday parties and anniversaries,

In the living room and kitchen.

It's the back-yard barbecue with friends,

Neighbors, and family connections.

It's the high school and college graduation,

And wedding receptions.

It's the family nights and block parties,

And the fellowship of family reunions.

Homeownership: It's more than real estate,

Land, brick and mortar, wood frame construction

And chicken wire.

It's more than the money saved,

Gifts and grants received.

It's more than the debt you incur to buy it.

It's more than the payments you make to own it.

It's more than the appreciation that comes,

With keeping it over time.

It's memories, it's family, and it's life,

That can happen in one place that you own,

Until you say it's time to move.

GOD IS GOOD AND GOD IS LOVE

ife is a journey and only God knows how it is going to end

And that is good thing.

I don't really want to know how it is going to end. Do you?

God knows and because God is good,

it is a good thing that He knows.

Because God is Good, and God is Love.

We are not in a tug of war with God.

His Love does not require us to compete for it.

Nor does He compete with us.

He is not against us.

He is not trying to stop us from being ourselves.

Because God is Good, and God is Love.

. . .

He is not trying to stop us from pursuing the desires of our heart.

Whether those pursuits are good or evil.

He is Good all the time. We are not.

He is God and He sees us as Good and Worthy of His attention.

He delights in all His creations including us.

Because God is Good, and God is Love.

We are the last of His creations and He declares us to be good.

God desires to be in a harmonious relationship with us.

He is purposing us and showering us with Gifts and life experiences.

That we could never obtain on our own.

He is Love and He loves us far above what we can conceive or believe.

Because God is Good, and God is Love.

He is God, He is Love, He is Good,

He is the Alpha and the Omega

He is the creator, our creator and made us in His image.

He loves us Because He loves Himself and He is Love.

Because God is Good, and God is Love.

So, as we take this journey, we know that we are not alone.

Nor do we need to be afraid because God is good, and God is love.

This is our mantra that gets us through the day,

When it seems like, God is not there or that we have lost our way.

And are left to deal with our problems on our own.

We say God is Good and God is love and we are Home.

Our feelings of abandonment are born out of the flesh which is weak and dying every day.

Our spirit always confirms His presence in our lives because God is Spirit, and He abides in Us.

His presence is confirmed by the Spirit, the Spirit that God has given us and that gives us life.

The body is dead absent the spirit. We are spirit and life and we are loved.

So, we walk boldly in this life facing our challenges,

As if they have already been met.

Because God is Good, and God is Love.

Attacking our problems as if they have already been solved.

Because we are loved and He who loved us is God

The creator of everything, In this life, and the life to come.

We are spirit, flesh and soul and will never die,

but will be changed, In form, and substance, to be with Him,

Because God is Good, and God is Love.

When He is ready to bring us a new beginning with a new journey on that day.

Not limited by space or time, or material things of any kind.

But to exist like He exists,

And to be one with Him in everything.

We will know that we are loved,

Because God is Good, and God is Love.

I AM NOT YOUR NIGGA

❦

I am not your Nigga

I love you too, and I know we are brothers, but I am not your nigga. Before I was given that name my people were kings and queens, men of courage and valor and distinction. My people were astronomers and builders and doctors and leaders. My people were free.

I am not your nigga. I love you too and I know we are brothers, but I am not your nigga. My captors, my owners, my enslaver, my dehumanizers gave me that name and appropriately so because I was less valuable than their sheep and pigs ready for the slaughterhouse. I was a nigga. Less than human, brought here chained to the bottom of a ship and forced to lay in my own feces. Dumped in the ocean as food for the shark when I died or was killed and dumped when I rebelled. Subjugation and dehumanization were my first and last name, but my enslaver just called me nigga.

I am not your nigga, I love you too and yes, we are brothers, but I am not your nigga. I was unmercifully dragged kicking and screaming from my homeland, in chains, robbed of my name, my culture, my identity, captured like an animal being prepared for the slaughter by my enslavers. I was worked to death and if not worked to death I was tortured and beaten to death. Mutilated, castrated, decapitated, and hung on trees for all the world to see.

I am not your nigga. I am not your negro. I am not your

African, af, ape, béni-oui-oui, bluegum, boogie, buck, burrhead, colored, coon, crow, eggplant, fuzzies, fuzzy-wuzzy, golliwogg, Bugaloo. I am not your monkey. I am not your darky. Jigaboo, jiggabo, jijjiboo, zigabo, jig, jigg, jiggy, jigga, Jungle bunny, Kaffir, kaffer, kafir, kaffre, mammy, mosshead, pickaninny, monkey, mosshead, munt, nignog, nigger, niger, nig , nigor , nigra, nigre, nigar, niggur, nigga, nigg , nigz , niggah, niggar, niggaz, nigguh, niggress, nigette, niglet, nigglet, nigra, negra, niggra, nigrah, nigruh, pickaninny, porch monkey, powder burn, quashie, sambo, smoked Irishman, sooty, spade, spook, tar baby, teapot, thicklips, and bootlips.

I love you too and yes, we are brothers, but I am not your nigga.

From 1816 in tobacco fields of Virginia to 1863 and the emancipation proclamation by President Lincoln, I was and still am a nigga.

The 13th Amendment: Abolished slavery and involuntary servitude, except as a punishment for a crime. Approved by the 38th Congress (1863–1865) as S.J. Res. 16, ratified by the states on December 6th, 1865 and yet I am still a nigga.

Civil Rights Act of 1866: Guaranteed all citizens' rights to make and enforce contracts and to purchase, sell, or lease property and passed by the 39th Congress (1865–1867) as S.R. 61 and yet I am still a nigga can buy or sell.

Fourteenth Amendment 1867: Declared that all persons born or naturalized in the U.S. were citizens and that any state that denied or abridged the voting rights of males over the age of 21 would be subject to proportional reductions in its representation in the U.S. House of Representatives. Approved by the 39th Congress (1865–1867) as H.J. Res. 127, ratified by the states on July 9th, 1868. They continue to prevent me from voting because and I am still a nigga.

The fifteenth Amendment 1869: Forbade any state to deprive a citizen of his vote because of race, color, or previous condition of servitude. Approved by the 40th Congress (1867–1869) as S.J. Res. 8, ratified by the states on February 3rd, 1870. Yet the fight to vote rages on because I am still a nigga.

First Ku Klux Klan Act (Civil Rights Act of 1870): Prohibited discrimination in voter registration based on race, color, or previous servitude condition. Established penalties for interfering with a person's right to vote. Gave federal courts the power to enforce the act and employ federal marshals and the army to uphold it. It was passed by the 41st Congress (1869–1871) as H.R. 1293. I am still threaten and deterred because I am still a nigga.

The Second Ku Klux Klan Act (Civil Rights Act of 1871): Placed all the north and South elections under federal control. It allowed for the appointment of election supervisors by federal circuit judges. Authorized U.S. Marshals to employ deputies to maintain order at polling places. It was passed by the 41st Congress (1869–1871) as H.R. 2634. Even with the protection of US Marshals I can't vote because I am still a nigga.

The third Ku Klux Klan Act (1871): Enforced the 14th Amendment by guaranteeing all citizens of the United States the Constitution's rights and provided legal protection under the Law. Passed by the 42nd Congress (1871–1873). Really? How many unarmed men have to die under the law of equal protection? I am still a nigga.

Civil Rights Act of 1875: Barred discrimination in public accommodations and on public conveyances on land and water. Prohibited exclusion of African Americans from jury duty. It was passed by the 43rd Congress (1873–1875) as H.R. 796. Even with a jury of my peers I am still a nigga.

The Civil Rights Act of 1957 created the six-member Commission on Civil Rights and established the Civil Rights Division in the U.S. Department of Justice. Authorized the U.S. Attorney General to seek court injunctions against deprivation and obstruction of voting rights by state officials. It was passed by the 85th Congress (1957–1959) as H.R. 6127. In Georgia and just about in any state in South I am still a nigga that they do not want to vote.

Civil Rights Act of 1960: Expanded the enforcement powers of the Civil Rights Act of 1957 and introduced criminal penalties for obstructing the implementation of federal court orders. They extended the Civil Rights Commission for two years and required that voting and registration records for federal elections be preserved. It was passed by the 86th Congress (1959–1961) as H.R. 8601. Yet I am still a nigga dealing with obstructions and obstacles with limited opportunity to vote.

The Civil Rights Act of 1964: Prohibited discrimination in public accommodations, facilities, and schools. Outlawed discrimination in federally funded projects. It created the Equal Employment Opportunity Commission to monitor employment discrimination in the public and private sectors and provided additional capacities to enforce voting rights. It extended the Civil Rights Commission for four years. It was passed by the 88th Congress (1963–1965) as H.R. 7152. Yet I am still a nigga and can't get job or an education because of discrimination.

The Voting Rights Act of 1965: suspended the use of literacy tests and voter disqualification devices for five years. Authorized the use of federal examiners to supervise voter registration in states that used tests or in which less than half the voting-eligible residents registered or voted. It directed the U.S. Attorney General to institute proceedings against the use of poll taxes. It provided criminal penalties for individuals who violated the act—passed by the 89th Congress (1965–1967) as S. 1564. Why is this necessary? Because America still sees me as just a nigga. They will need the threat of federal prison to allow us **to vote.**

The Civil Rights Act of 1968 (Fair Housing Act): prohibited discrimination in the sale or rental of approximately 80 percent of the housing in the U.S. Prohibited state governments and native-American tribal governments from violating the constitutional rights of native Americans. It was passed by the 90th Congress (1967–1969) as H.R. 2516. Yet deed and covenant restriction continued to deny my right to housing because I am still a nigga and can't buy a home or live where I want to live.

Voting Rights Act Amendments of 1970: Extended the provisions of the Voting Rights Act of 1965 for five years. Made the act applicable to areas where less than 50 percent of the eligible voting-age population registered as of november 1968. It was passed by the 91st Congress (1969–1971) as H.R. 4249. Why are we still dealing with this? Because I am still a nigga and the right to vote is not for me.

Voting Rights Act Amendments of 1975: Extended the provisions of the Voting Rights Act of 1965 for seven years. Established coverage for other minority groups, including native Americans, Hispanic Americans, and Asian Americans. Permanently banned literacy tests. Passed by the 94th Congress (1975–1977) as H.R. 6219. Why the resistance? Because I am still a nigga and the right to vote is not for me.

Voting Rights Act Amendments of 1982: Extended for 25 years the provisions of the Voting Rights Act of 1965. Allowed jurisdictions that could provide evidence of maintaining a clean voting rights record for at least ten years, to avoid preclearance coverage (the requirement of federal approval of any change to local or state voting laws). Provided aid and instruction to disabled or illiterate voters. Provided bilingual election materials in jurisdictions with large minority populations. Passed by the 97th Congress (1981–1983) as H.R. 3112. Yet I am still a nigga. My disability, illiteracy, inability to speak the language is my problem and another reason to take away my vote.

Civil Rights Restoration Act of 1987: Established that anti-discrimination laws apply to an entire organization if any part of the organization receives federal funds. It was passed by the 100th Congress (1987–1989) as S. 557. Yet I am still a nigga dealing with Federal funded discrimination through organizations.

Fair Housing Act Amendments of 1988: Strengthened the powers of enforcement granted to the Housing and Urban Development Department in the 1968 Fair Housing Act and passed by the 100th Congress (1987–1989) as H.R. 1158. Yet I am still a nigga and housing discrimination is the game they play.

The Civil Rights Act of 1991: Reversed nine U.S. Supreme Court decisions (rendered between 1986 and 1991) raised the bar for workers who alleged job discrimination—provided for plaintiffs to receive monetary damages in cases of harassment or discrimination based on sex, religion, or disability—passed by the 102nd Congress (1991–1993) as S. 1745. Yet I am still a nigga and job, gender and religious discrimination are the games they play.

Voting Rights Act of 2006: Extended the provisions of the Voting Rights Act of 1965 for 25 years. It extended the bilingual election requirements through August 5th, 2032. Directed the U.S. Comptroller General to study and report to Congress on the implementation, effectiveness, and efficiency of bilingual voting materials requirements. It was passed by the 109th Congress (2005–2007) as H.R. 9. We are a nation of immigrants, and everyone is learning english to vote. We need to get out the Black vote.

Thank God we are a country of Laws! The Supreme Court is where we fight for our cause. Our state governments allow racism to be their law and require the wisdom of men and women who are the final arbitrators of the Law. Where would it be without Federal intervention living in states seeking conflict among the races and division. Thank God for Abraham Lincoln.

Juneteenth should have the same significance in the world, and the United States, as the 4th of July. On July 2nd, 1776, the Continental Congress voted in favor of independence, and two days later, delegates from the 13 colonies adopted the Declaration of Independence, a historic document drafted by Thomas Jefferson. From 1776 to the present day, July 4th is celebrated as the birth of American independence but not ours.

Juneteenth should be recognized as a Federal Holiday to represent the birth of African American independence. My African Ancestors gave their lives as slaves. Their children, grandchildren, and great children have suffered from slavery. This is the right thing to do in America.

Ostracized from society because of the color of my skin, my heritage and, my hair. Segregated, humiliated and, denied access to anything white. From pools, to hotels, restaurants to theaters, streets to whole neighborhoods. Due to racial divides, I had to hide—had to keep my black behind in the Hood if I knew what was good — because to them I am a nigga.

I am not your nigga. I love you too, and yes, we are brothers, but I am not your Nigga.

QUIT

Quit and you will Die

Not a physical death

But as aspirational death

An emotional and spiritual death

Quit becomes who you are

Quit becomes your song and mantra

Quit becomes our mindset and belief system

Quit becomes your goal for every project you never achieve

Quit becomes every destination you never arrived

Quit becomes every commitment you always break

Quit becomes every promise you fail to keep

Quit becomes every marriage that ends in divorce.

Because you quit. You Quit!

. . .

You Quit in your mind

You Quit in your heart

You quit in your dreams

You quit in your hopes

You quit in your voice

You quit in you posture

You quit in your face

You quit in your appearance

You quit in your hygiene

You quit is written all over you

You smell like quit

You talk like quit

You act like quit

Because you Quit is who you are.

Quit is profane. It is a four-letter word

Straight from the bowels of hell pregnant with death

And ready to give birth to failure and depression and guilt and anger

And every foul thing that only death can wreak of.

Don't quit if that is not who you are

Your purpose is not to quit and to explain why but to proclaim how
you overcame

You purpose is not quit but to push on because quit is not who
you are.

There is no quit when there are no excuses.

There is no quit when there is no plan B

There is no quit when there is commitment

There is no quit when there is honor

There is no quit when there is humility

There is no quit when there is a willingness to adapt

There is no quit when there is a willingness to adjust

There is no quit when there is duty to succeed

There is not quit when there are obligations to keep

There is no quit when failure is not an option

There is no quit when you are too busy in the relentless pursuit

There is not quit when you are too dedicated to think about alternatives

There is no quit when there is a singleness of mind

There is no quit when there is a solid plan and near flawless execution

There is no quit because that is not who you are.

Who are you?

Powerful, Beautiful, Intelligent, Capable of anything you put your mind to accomplish.

Created in the image of God

Wonderfully made and divinely equipped

You are Man and Woman

With gifts and talents and ability that Only God could have endowed.

. . .

God does not do quit. He never has. He just does....

He creates, and sustains and never fails because

He never quits being God.

Be the man or woman you were created to be

And Be the Imagine of God

And Don't quit.

THE POWER IS NOW

*T*he Power Is Now

I believe that power is now because now is all I have right now.

This very hour, minute or second. In this special moment of time, I am a participant in the divine power that makes time a reality.

Everything I do, everything I think or say originate from the power that enables my consciousness to move me forward into action or inaction.

To participation or observation. To peace or chaos. To love or hate. To courage or fear. To life or death.

My power is now. Your power is now. Our power collectively is now. The power is now and essence of my existence.

Now represents eternity in the divine rim. It has no beginning or ending. Now just is. We see minutes, hours, and seconds because of our mortality.

Our human condition is frail and weak, and we are dying a little bit every day. We desire sleep and rest, food and water, love, and companionship.

And we see the end of our days, but it all just daily new beginnings of life until now becomes eternity. And we participate in the divine rim where there are no sunrises nor sunsets, just now and knowing who we really are. The power is now!

DID YOU ENJOY THIS BOOK?

I sure hope so!

Please join our family and write a review. Reviews are the "tip jar" of the book publishing industry. New readers weigh reviews heavily in deciding to make a purchase. You being so generous as to share your experience is the lifeblood of the success of "The Power Poetry Collection".

I appreciate you!
Eric Lawrence Frazier

SCAN ME

THE POWER IS NOW MEDIA

The Power Is Now Media is an online multimedia company founded in 2009 by Eric L. Frazier MBA, headquartered in Riverside, California. We are advocates for homeownership, wealth building, and financial literacy. We create and publish original educational content about real estate through nationally syndicated Radio, Podcasts, Magazines, TV, Social Media, Streaming platforms, and special online seminars and webinars. We are an online platform and resource for everyone to learn about homeownership, housing, loan programs, and down payment assistance to achieve financial literacy and the American dream of homeownership. We are supported by housing finance agencies, real estate associations, and civic, religious, and community organizations. We help them amplify their voice about the services and programs they offer in lending, housing, and homeownership. Visit us at www.thepowerisnow.com

The Mission of the Power is Now Media is to inspire and educate consumers and real estate professionals to build wealth through the acquisition, management, and sale of real estate with information and support we provide via our website, live and on-demand TV, and social media platforms that empower everyone to own real estate now and achieve the American dream of homeownership. Our company slogan is "We are leading the conversation about real homeownership."

The Power Is Now Media corporate office is located at 3739 6th Street, Riverside, CA 92501. Telephone/Fax: 800-401-8994. Eric Lawrence Frazier MBA is a California Licensed Loan Originator (NMLS License #461807) and Real Estate Broker (License #O1148434).

ABOUT THE AUTHOR

Mr. Eric Lawrence Frazier MBA is the President, and CEO of The Power Is Now Media, The Power Is Now is a multimedia company that specializes in real estate education for consumers and real estate professionals on various topics in real estate, lending, economics, and government policy. The information is published on The Power Is Now Media website (www.thepowerisnow.com), national online radio and podcast platforms nationwide, Major social media channels, and live-stream TV platforms.

Mr. Frazier is also the publisher and editor-in-chief of The Power Is Now Magazines, which are online real estate magazines first published on September 1, 2013. These magazines focus on real estate education, real estate homes for sale, and national real estate news. Mr. Frazier is a graduate of Redlands University in Redlands, California, and has an MBA with an emphasis in finance and a BS in business administration and management. He has lectured at the University of California Riverside on the US mortgage crisis to international business leaders from India and has served as an adjunct professor.

With nearly four decades of originations, management, underwriting, operations, and marketing experience, Mr. Frazier is nationally known as a mortgage lending professional. He has over thirty years of experience in real estate sales as a licensed California real estate agent and over twenty years of experience as a real estate broker (#01143484).

He and his wife are the founders of Frazier Group Reality. (fraziergrouprealty.com), a-full-service,family-owned-and-operated real estate company in Riverside, California. Mr. Frazier is the former president of the Orange County Realtist, which was a chapter of the National Association of Real Estate Brokers (NAREB), and former director of the California Association of Real Estate Brokers. He is a former vice president of the Orange County National Association of Hispanic Real Estate Professionals and a former advisory board member of the Orange County Asian Real Estate Association of America.

He is also on the board of directors of the Riverside Fair Housing Council; the board of directors of Project Tomorrow (tomorrow.org), a national education nonprofit; a member of the 100 Black Men of America and the NAACP; a pastor; and leader of The Power Is Now Ministries. He is a member of the National Association of Mortgage Brokers, the Pacific West Realtors Association of Realtors, the California Association of Realtors (CAR), and the National Association of Realtors (NAR). He is the past president and director of the State of California African American Museum (www.caamuseum.org) and a former pastor of the North Fontana Church.

Mr. Frazier is also an author, singer, poet, and songwriter. He is a blogger, motivational speaker, business consultant, business coach for profit and non profit companies, and community leader. He enjoys golf, running, and jazz music. Mr. Frazier strives to be a role model for African American men and enjoys mentoring and coaching young people and adults. His greatest accomplishments are being married to the love of his life for over forty years and being the father of four daughters. His three oldest daughters have master's degrees in management and business, and his youngest daughter has a bachelor's degree in apparel merchandising and management. All of Mr. Frazier's accomplishments and associations can be found at www.linkedin.com/in/ericfrazier.

FOLLOW ME ON SOCIAL MEDIA

LET'S CONNECT ON LINKEDIN

www.ingramcontent.com/pod-product-compliance
Lightning Source LLC
Chambersburg PA
CBHW032046040426
42449CB00007B/1004